Roger FEDERER

By Ellen Labrecque

The Child's World®
www.childsworld.com

Published in the United States of America by The Child's World®
1980 Lookout Drive • Mankato, MN 56003-1705
800-599-READ • www.childsworld.com

ACKNOWLEDGMENTS

The Child's World®: Mary Berendes, Publishing Director

Produced by Shoreline Publishing Group LLC
President / Editorial Director: James Buckley, Jr.
Designer: Tom Carling, carlingdesign.com
Assistant Editor: Jim Gigliotti

Photo Credits: Cover: Stuart Franklin/Getty Images.
Interior: AP/Wide World: 5, 10, 13, 18, 21, 22, 28; Corbis: 16; Getty
Images: 1, 3, 7, 8, 15, 25, 27.

LIBRARY OF CONGRESS
CATALOGING-IN-PUBLICATION DATA

Labrecque, Ellen.
  Roger Federer / by Ellen Labrecque.
     p. cm. — (The world's greatest athletes)
  Includes index.
  ISBN 978-1-59296-882-4 (library bound : alk. paper)
 1. Federer, Roger, 1981– 2. Tennis players—Switzerland—
Biography. 3. Tennis. I. Title. II. Series.

  GV994.F43L33 2008
  796.342092—dc22

                                        2007031993

CONTENTS

INTRODUCTION
On Top of the World 4
CHAPTER 1
The Young Swiss Sensation 6
CHAPTER 2
From Young Star to Pro 12
CHAPTER 3
And Now . . . Simply the Best 18
CHAPTER 4
Roger Keeps Rolling Along 24

CAREER TOTALS 29
GLOSSARY 30
FIND OUT MORE 31
INDEX AND ABOUT THE AUTHOR 32

On Top of the World

HOW GREAT IS TENNIS PLAYER ROGER FEDERER? Before answering that question, let's go back and study his performance at the Australian Open in January, 2007.

Roger cruised through that **Grand Slam** tournament without breaking a sweat. Roger clobbered former No. 1-ranked Andy Roddick in straight **sets** in the semifinals. Roddick described the **match** as "an absolute beating." In the final against Fernando Gonzalez of Chile, the "Mighty Fed" **prevailed** in straight sets again. Roger became the first man to win a Grand Slam tournament without dropping a set since legendary Bjorn Borg at the 1980 French Open. At the age of 25, Roger won his 10th Grand Slam title at the Australian Open. The great

Pete Sampras, who holds the career record of 14 Grand Slam titles, didn't win his 10th until he was a month shy of 27 years old.

Throughout Roger's matches at the Australian Open, a fan held up a sign that read, "Quiet: Genius at Work." Genius, indeed. The superstar finished the 2006 season ranked No. 1 in the world for the third year in a row. He also won 12 tournaments in '06. That was the most by a player in a season since 1995. As of September 2007, Roger was still ranked first in the world.

Now, armed with these facts, it is easier to answer the question, "How great is Roger Federer?"

"I mean, look, I guess I'm the best tennis player in the world," Roger said after his Australian win.

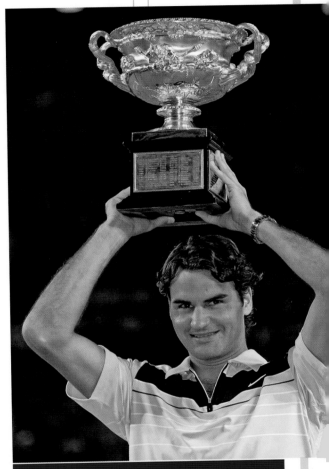

This happens a lot: Roger holds up another championship trophy.

The genius is *almost* right. He is the best in the world *today*. But, many experts think that he also happens to be the greatest player *ever* in the history of the game.

CHAPTER 1

The Young Swiss Sensation

ROGER FEDERER WAS BORN IN BASEL, SWITZERLAND, on August 8, 1981. His mother, Lynette, is from South Africa. His father, Robert, is Swiss. Roger has one sister, Diana, who is two years older than he is.

When Roger was a young child, his mom and dad took him to their local tennis club in Basel. At first, while his parents played tennis, he would run around and play hide-and-seek. But when Roger was three, he picked up a tennis racquet. "He loved the sport from the beginning," his mom said.

Roger used the racquet to hit a tennis ball against a wall, against a cupboard, or even against the garage door. He was a natural. Lynette says her son's hand-eye coordination was exceptional, even at such an early age.

Roger has had a tennis racquet in his hand almost every day since he first picked one up when he was three years old.

"He couldn't even see over the table-tennis table, but he could hit the ball over the net," Lynette told *Sports Illustrated*. "People kept telling me he was amazing."

Roger didn't love just tennis as a child, though. He loved all sports. He could always be found playing something, especially soccer or tennis.

"I loved playing with balls, whatever sport they were from: ping pong, tennis, basketball, soccer," Roger said about his childhood days. "I was always trying something."

Although Roger tried other competitions, tennis was the sport he took the most seriously. At age six, he attended tennis clinics. In 1989, Roger's mother signed him up for a **prestigious** junior program at the TC Old Boys Club in a town called Binningen, which

That's Roger's dad, Robert, and his mom, Lynette, posing with him at an awards banquet in 2005.

was just outside of Basel. It was Roger's first step to becoming a star.

The program at the Old Boys Club allowed Roger to get one-on-one coaching for the first time. From the ages of 8 to 14, his two main coaches were Adolf "Seppli" Kavovski and Peter Carter. Seppli did most of the one-on-one instruction, while Peter coached the entire junior squad. Seppli knew Roger would be a star from the first time he saw him play.

"After one or two days, I knew he was a massive talent," Seppli said. "After two days, I knew Roger was born with a racquet in his hands."

As Roger's game improved, his attitude also became more and more intense. He never liked to lose. Sometimes, he would throw his racquet or scream at himself in frustration. On occasion, he would also cry. Sometimes his parents, who were sitting in the stands, would yell at their son to settle down, but that only made Roger more upset.

"I used to get so angry and frustrated," Roger said about his young playing days. "I knew what I could do, and failure made me mad. I would just explode."

Despite such outbursts, Roger blossomed into an amazing player. In 1992, he was ranked No. 2 in

In 2007, Roger broke former tennis great Jimmy Connors' record of 160 consecutive weeks atop the men's tennis rankings.

his age group in Switzerland. A year later, he won the Swiss under-12 national championship.

Roger and his parents soon felt it was time to take his game to the next level. In 1995, at age 14, Roger enrolled in the Swiss national training center in Ecublens, Switzerland. Ecublens was in a different part of the country than Basel. Roger had to live apart from his family at the training center, where he also attended school, for five days a week. At first, he was homesick and didn't like his home away from home.

Roger can still get emotional, but now he controls his anger on the court.

"I was not happy," Roger said of that time. "I used to cry when I had to leave on Sunday nights to go back."

Despite Roger's unhappiness, training at the center improved his game a lot. His strokes became more smooth and his footwork helped him become more **agile**. It was starting to look more and more like he had the talent to become a **professional**.

Young Roger

As a 12-year-old, Roger was almost as good at soccer as he was at tennis. He played for a club team in Basel. "I'm convinced that if he'd chosen soccer, he'd have made it to the Swiss national team," says Seppli Kavovski, Roger's tennis coach. When Roger had to choose between soccer and tennis, of course, he chose tennis.

In the mid-1990s, when Roger was in his early teens, he was a ball boy at the Swiss Indoors ATP (Association of Tennis Professionals) event and at a women's professional event in his area. He met some of the big stars of the day, such as fellow Swiss Martina Hingis. Little did Roger know, he would be one of those big stars in just a few short years.

As a boy, Roger was known to have a fun, outgoing personality. He was always cracking jokes and trying to make his friends laugh. At tennis practice, he would hit a great smash and announce, "That's the shot I'm going to win Wimbledon with." Roger was joking at the time, but he wasn't far from the truth.

Roger's on-the-court attitude, though, remained fiery. He still threw his racquet and screamed at himself frequently.

It was clear to his parents and his coaches that he needed a few more years to **mature** before he turned pro.

Roger has represented his country in international play since 1997. Here, he carries the Swiss flag in the 2004 Olympics.

CHAPTER 2

From Young Star to Pro

THE YEAR 1997, WHEN ROGER WAS 15 GOING ON 16, was a big one for the young Swiss. He made his international debut, representing his country in the World Youth Cup that was held in Zurich, Switzerland. Roger beat a young Australian, Lleyton Hewitt (who also went on to become a highly ranked pro). Next, Roger moved from Ecublens to Biel, Switzerland, to train at a new center opened by the Swiss Tennis Association. Peter Carter, Roger's team coach from the Old Boys Club, joined Roger in Biel. But the biggest change Roger made in 1997 was to give up his formal schooling and concentrate solely on tennis.

In 1998, Roger played his first and only full year of top junior events. He made it to the semifinals of the Australian Open Junior tournament, and he lost in the early rounds of the French Junior Open. He won the Wimbledon Junior Title in England, and made the finals at the U.S. Open Juniors. He also won several other smaller tournaments throughout his junior tour. By the end of the season, Roger's results

In His Own Words

Roger had a terrible temper as a young player growing up. He says:

▶ *"I was a terrible loser," Roger said. "I screamed. I swore. I threw my racquet. I acted bad. I started to feel embarrassed at times, you know, playing on center court and throwing my racquet, breaking them and hitting balls all over the place. And so I stopped, and became really focused on the game instead."*

Today, Roger is known for his cool and calm demeanor. But he says most of the time it is an act.

▶ *"I may wear a poker face, but trust me, I get nervous inside."*

The key to Roger's success is his ability to hit a variety of shots. Most players just rely on power; his game is more of a mixed bag.

▶ *"I play very classical tennis. I use a lot of **topspin** on my forehand. I have to mix up my game because my opponents are very hard hitters."*

Roger was only 17 years old when he first competed at the prestigious French Open (above) in May of 1999.

were impressive enough for him to be named the world junior champion.

The following season, Roger planned to turn pro. But first, he knew he had to learn how to control his temper. On the junior tour, he was throwing his racquet and yelling at himself. Sometimes, he would even cry during matches, just as he did when he was a boy.

"I knew that when I went to the big venues, such as Wimbledon, and when I played the top men, I couldn't behave like that," Roger said.

So, on his last days of the junior circuit, he hired a **psychologist**. Throughout the next year, the psychologist helped Roger control his anger and focus his energy in a more positive direction—toward

Pete Sampras (left) was on a big winning streak until Roger recorded a stunning upset at Wimbledon in 2001.

winning. When Roger turned pro in 1998, he had become a calm, focused player who was not easily rattled or bothered.

Roger showed amazing promise on his first couple of years on the ATP Tour. In 1998, he advanced to the quarterfinals of a tournament in Toulouse, France. It was just his second ATP event. He finished the 1999 season as the youngest player (at 18 years, 4 months) that year in the Top 100 of the ATP Rankings. In 2000, he lost in the bronze medal match of the 2000 Summer Olympics in Sydney, Australia.

By 2001, Roger was really coming into his own. He won his first ATP title in Milan, Italy. But the biggest win of his career came in the fourth round at the 2001 Wimbledon tournament against top-seeded Pete Sampras, who was riding a 31-match winning streak. Playing on Centre Court (the main court), Federer defeated the defending champion in five sets.

"There are a lot of young guys coming up," Sampras said, "but Roger is a bit extra-special."

Roger still lost in the next round, but it didn't seem to matter. The 19-year-old had made his mark by beating the former No. 1 player in the world. He was on his way to the top.

When Roger won at Wimbledon in 2007, he equaled Bjorn Borg's modern-era record of five consecutive men's singles titles there.

Roger has been reaching for the top since he began his tennis career. By 2004, he ascended to No. 1 in the rankings.

CHAPTER 3

And Now . . . Simply the Best

ON PAPER, THE 2002 SEASON WAS A SUCCESSFUL one for Roger. He captured three ATP titles, reached five tournament finals, and finished the season sixth in the rankings. It was the highest finish of his career. But 2002 was also a year **marred** by tragedy. Peter Carter, Roger's former coach and close friend, was killed in a car accident in early August. Roger was devastated by the news.

"It was terrible," Roger said. "I never really lost a friend out of the blue like that. I was really sad. It's still hard to find words to describe how it feels."

After mourning for months, Roger decided to use the tragedy as motivation to become an even better player. He knew that is what Coach Carter would have wanted.

"His death put everything in perspective," Roger said. "I fought a lot. I came out stronger."

Filled with fresh fire in 2003, Roger was close to unstoppable. He won an ATP-high seven titles. He finished the season ranked No. 2 in the world. It was the sixth straight season he had improved his year-end ranking. Roger's biggest win of the season came when he defeated Australian Mark Philippoussis in the finals of Wimbledon. The victory was Roger's first Grand Slam title. When the match ended, Roger broke down on his knees and sobbed. Afterwards, he only wanted to speak about Coach Carter.

"We would have had a big party together if he was still here," Roger said. "I'm sure he was watching the match from somewhere."

If 2003 was the year Roger was *close* to unstoppable, then 2004 was the year he *was* unstoppable. The Swiss superstar captured an ATP-best 11 titles in as many finals. He won three Grand Slam events—the Australian Open, Wimbledon, and the U.S Open. He finished the season as the No. 1-ranked player in the world. He was just 23 years old and the first male player from Switzerland ever to be top-ranked in the sport.

Roger beats his opponents with a style that is different from most other top players of his day. Usually, the men's game is won by power. The player

After winning at Wimbledon in 2003, Roger wept in memory of his former coach and friend, Peter Carter.

with the fastest serve, and the biggest forehand, dominates. Roger, on the other hand, overwhelms opponents with a bundle of resources.

"He can beat different guys different ways," says tennis great Andre Agassi. "He does everything really good, and a few things really great."

Roger's excellent footwork, which enables him to get to balls that many other players can't, helps set him apart.

Helping Hands

Roger's first love is tennis, but when he isn't playing, he loves to help people, especially children. In December 2003, Roger established the Roger Federer Foundation (RFF). The Foundation aids poor children in South Africa, the home country of Roger's mother. The RFF pays school fees for hundreds of children, provides them with a warm meal each day, and helps pay teacher's salaries.

"I believe all children deserve the chance to make something of their lives," says Roger. "This is the mission behind my Foundation."

Thanks to Roger, more and more children get this chance every day.

One of Roger's greatest strengths is his footwork: He never seems out of place, and he chases down balls that other players deem "ungettable." He mixes in **drop shots**, topspin, and **slices** all the time. Roger is like an artist who paints with a fine brush, while opponents appear to be working with a paint roller.

"Roger's a magician," says fellow pro Marat Safin of Russia.

Women's star Serena Williams of the United States summed up Roger's 2004 performance even better. "I wish I could play like Roger Federer," she said simply. Most other pro tennis players felt exactly the same way.

Roger Keeps Rolling Along

IT DOESN'T SEEM POSSIBLE, BUT ROGER'S GAME has continued to improve since he reached the top in 2004. In 2005, he finished ranked No. 1 in the world for the second straight season. He won an ATP-best 11 titles, including two more Grand Slam tournaments. In 2006, he again finished in first and won an ATP-best 12 titles, including three more Grand Slam tournaments. Roger's record from 2004 to 2006 was a remarkable 247 wins and just 15 losses. Most impressively, his victories in 2007 at the Australian Open, Wimbledon, and the U.S. Open gave him 12 wins in the last 17 Grand Slam events.

"There's no one who can play with him," Pete Sampras said in late 2005. "For the next four or five years, his competition will be the record books."

Roger became No. 1 in the world in 2004, but he didn't let up. He was still atop the rankings through 2007.

Although it does seem that Roger's game is in a class by itself, there is one player who puts Roger to the test when they face off: lefthanded Rafael Nadal of Spain. Nadal is the world's No. 2-ranked player. He is the only active player who has a winning record against Roger.

"Federer is in a new position," said retired player Mats Wilander, a three-time French Open champion. "He has to answer the question [about Nadal]. 'How can I beat this guy?'"

Here is what some of Roger's opponents and former players have to say about the world's No. 1 player:

▶ *"He might be the smoothest, most talented player I've ever laid eyes on."* –John McEnroe, former pro player and current tennis commentator

▶ *"I threw the kitchen sink at him, but he went to the bathroom and got a tub."* –Andy Roddick, after losing to Roger in the 2004 Wimbledon final

▶ *"He's setting the standard for everyone right now. He's so difficult because he's so complete."* –Pro tennis player Tim Henman

In terms of style, the two players couldn't be any different. Nadal's best playing surface is clay, while Roger prefers grass or hardcourt. Also, Nadal is a power player. He hits blazing cross-court slams and pounds away from the baseline. Roger uses a variety of shots. He likes to approach the net as much as he likes hitting from the baseline. What Roger's game lacks in power, though, he makes up for in creativity.

This style has left many other opponents confused, but not Nadal. Rafael, who is five years younger than Roger, uses the same game plan every time he plays the Swiss. He hits deep, hard shots to Roger's backhand—the weakest of Federer's strokes. Nadal also whizzes **passing shots** by Roger when he approaches the net. But Nadal's most important ingredient in his winning recipe is his belief that he can win.

"You need to believe about victory," Nadal told *Sports Illustrated*. "Some players, when they play [Roger], they don't believe. But I believe in victory, always. I know it's not impossible."

Nadal holds the edge in head-to-head competition, but Roger recently reestablished his authority in a thrilling, five-set match at the 2007 Wimbledon final.

"He's better than me," said Nadal. "You can see the numbers, you can see the details."

Rafael Nadal (below) gives Roger some of his toughest matches.

In truth, Roger isn't just better than Nadal. He is better in tennis than anybody else on the planet. Nadal is a **formidable** rival, especially on clay. For now, though, Roger doesn't have any steady competition.

In 2007, Roger's fifth straight Wimbledon title tied a record.

"Roger's game makes it look as if his side of the court is smaller and the opponent's side is bigger," wrote Swiss journalist Freddy Widmer, "and that he has more time to play his shots than his opponent."

If Roger keeps playing the way he is, he'll have to look inward for motivation, because opponents won't be able to stop him. Like Tiger Woods in golf, when Roger is on, nobody can beat him.

"To me, Roger Federer is the right model for anyone aspiring to be a tennis player," says Bjorn Borg. "It's such a pleasure to just watch him play. All records will tumble when it comes to Roger. He is such a complete player that I do not see anyone being better than him for a long time from now."

Roger Federer's Career Totals

Through September 2007

CURRENT ATP SINGLES RANKING: 1st

GRAND SLAM TITLES: 12

SINGLES RECORD: 535–131

SINGLES TITLES: 51

DOUBLES RECORD: 104–68

DOUBLES TITLES: 7

PRIZE MONEY: $35,640,078

GLOSSARY

agile able to move around the court more easily

drop shots tennis shots that drop softly just over the net

formidable strong, forceful, or powerful

Grand Slam one of four major tournaments on the men's and women's pro tennis tour; the four tournaments are the Australian Open, the French Open, Wimbledon, and the U.S. Open

marred spoiled or damaged

match a tennis competition

mature able to act properly for one's age

passing shots tennis shots that are hit past an opponent, usually when he or she is near the net

prestigious having a high reputation, respected

prevailed to have been greater in strength or influence; triumphed

professional a person who is paid to play a sport

psychologist a person trained to work with and study the human mind

sets in tennis, a group of games. The first player to win six games wins the set (tiebreakers kick in when the games are tied 5–5 or 6–6).

slices tricky tennis shots hit so that they spin and curve instead of going in a straight line

topspin when the ball is hit so that it rotates very quickly in the direction that it is traveling

FIND OUT MORE

BOOKS

Fantastic Federer
> By *Chris Bowers*
> London, England: John Blake Publishing, Ltd., 2007.
> A well-known tennis journalist explores how Roger Federer has made it to the top of his sport's rankings.

History of Sports—Tennis
> By *Victoria Sherrow*
> Chicago: Lucent Books, 2002.
> Want to see where Roger Federer fits in the history of tennis? This book takes young readers from the origins of the game to the decade of the 2000s.

How to Play Tennis
> By *Venus and Serena Williams*.
> New York: DK Publishing, 2004.
> Get valuable tennis tips from two of the top women's pros in this helpful book.

WEB SITES

Visit our Web page for lots of links about Roger Federer and tennis: www.childsworld.com/links

Note to Parents, Teachers, and Librarians: We routinely check our Web links to make sure they're safe, active sites—so encourage your readers to check them out!

INDEX

Association of Tennis Professionals (ATP), 11, 17, 19, 20, 21, 24
attitude, 17, 20. See also temper
Australian Open, 20, 24
Australian Open Junior, 14

Borg, Bjorn, 17, 28

career totals, 29
Carter, Peter, 9, 13, 19, 20, 21
charity activities, 23
childhood, 6–11

Federer, Diana (sister), 6
Federer, Lynette (mother), 6–7, 8

Federer, Robert (father), 6, 8
French Junior Open, 14
French Open, 15, 25

Grand Slam, 20, 24, 29

Kavovski, Adolf "Seppli", 9, 11

Nadal, Rafael, 25–28

Old Boys Club, 8–9
Olympic Games, 12, 17

record breaking, 9
Roger Federer Foundation (RFF), 23

Sampras, Pete, 16, 17, 24

Swiss Tennis Association, 13

teen years, 9, 10, 11, 13–17
temper, 9, 10, 11, 14, 15–16
tennis skills, 14, 22–23, 26
training, 8–9, 10, 13

U.S. Open, 20
U.S. Open Juniors, 14

Wimbledon, 16, 17, 20, 21, 24, 27, 28
Wimbledon Junior, 14
world rank, No. 1, 20, 24–25
World Youth Cup, 13

ABOUT THE AUTHOR

Ellen Labrecque is a former senior editor at *Sports Illustrated for Kids*. She wrote about numerous sports for the magazine and contributed to several SI Kids books. The author of two other books in this series, she lives in New Jersey with her husband.